A History of American Music

JAZZ

Christopher Handyside

Heinemann Library
Chicago, Illinois

© 2006 Heinemann Library
First published in paperback in 2007
a division of Reed Elsevier Inc.
Chicago, Illinois

Customer Service 888–454–2279
Visit our website at www.heinemannraintree.com

Photo research by Hannah Taylor, Maria Joannou,
and Erica Newbery
Designed by Philippa Baile and Ron Kamen
Printed in China by WKT Company Limited.

11 10 09 08 07
10 9 8 7 6 5 4 3 2 1

Library of Congress Cataloging-in-Publication Data
Handyside, Chris.
  Jazz / Christopher Handyside.
    p. cm. – (A history of American music)
  Includes bibliographical references and index.
ISBN 978 1 403 48149 8 (hc)
ISBN 978 0 431 05681 4 (pbk)
  1. Jazz–History and criticism–Juvenile literature. I.
Title. II.
Series.
  ML3506.H26 2006
  781.65'0973–dc22

                    2005019305

Acknowledgments
The author and publishers are grateful to the
following for permission to reproduce copyright
material:
Corbis/Bettmann pp. 5, 6, 7, 16–17, 20– 21; Corbis
pp. 43 (Henry Diltz), 33 (Marvin Koner);
Corbis/Underwood & Underwood p. 18; Getty
Images pp. 9 (MPI), 10–11, 14, 15, 19, 27, 28 (Hulton
Archive), 36 (Hulton Archive/Bob Parent), 23, 24, 30,
35 (Time & Life Pictures) 42 (Time & Life
Pictures/Ted Thai); Library of Congress pp. 8, 29; M.
Jones Archives/Jazz Index p. 20; Redferns pp. 12
(Max Jones files), 13 top (William Gotlieb), 38 (Tom
Hanley), 31 (Michael Ochs Archive), 13 bottom, 37
(Chuck Stewart); Rex pp. 40 (Globe Photos Inc.), 39
(Peter Sanders); Sony Music Entertainment/Jazz
Index p. 41; Verve Records/Jazz Index p. 22.

Cover photograph of a trumpet player
reproduced with permission of Rex/Sipa Press.

The publishers would like to thank Patrick Allen for
his assistance with the preparation of this book.

Every effort has been made to contact copyright
holders of any material reproduced in this book.
Any omissions will be rectified in subsequent
printings if notice is given to the publishers.

Words shown in **boldface** are defined in the
glossary on page 46.

Contents

What is Jazz Music?

Jazz music is a uniquely American art form. Over the course of its first 100-plus years, jazz has evolved from a loosely defined mix of influences into an artistic and cultural phenomenon that is popular around the world. Jazz can be straightforward and good for dancing, or it can be complex and confusing enough for even the most academic listener. Jazz has been called "America's classical music," and its story is a mirror of the story of America after the Civil War. Much like blues and rhythm and blues (R&B), the story of jazz is also uniquely tied to the history of African Americans.

So where did jazz come from? What makes a jazz song a jazz song? What is jazz music?

African roots

Jazz music began in New Orleans, Louisiana, as early as the 1890s. The first jazz records were made in 1917. But to trace the true roots of jazz, a person has to investigate the musical history of three continents.

The foundation of jazz owes a great debt to African, especially West African, music. Many of the slaves that were taken to America were originally from West Africa, and their music featured many characteristics that became typical of jazz. First among these was the **call-and-response** structure. One player would play a beat or a melody, and another player would imitate the first but slightly alter—or **improvise** on—the original. In fact, improvisation (when a musician creates music on the spot) is the cornerstone of jazz. It provides the exciting energy and creativity that has kept jazz alive for over a hundred years.

African music also gave jazz its rhythmic approach. Jazz is characterized by **syncopation**—when the beat of the music is temporarily changed to give emphasis to the rhythm. It also features **polyrhythm**. Polyrhythm is where one rhythm is played simultaneously with another. Both of these rhythmic patterns have their origins in West African communal music. Typical jazz instruments, such as the banjo and the drum, were also of African origin.

Jazz lovers outside one of Harlem's most famous jazz clubs, the Savoy, in 1945.

European roots

Once Africans became part of American culture, they were exposed to European instruments, such as the cornet, saxophone, piano, bass, and guitar. These instruments, together with the drums, became the tools for the development of jazz music. Jazz also borrowed some of its basic structures, such as harmony, from European classical music.

These jazz musicians are playing on instruments commonly used in European music.

North American roots

Jazz's roots in North America lie in many of the ideas that followed Africans to the New World with the slave trade. Once in America, African slaves were discouraged from congregating. Members of tribes were sold to different masters. They were forced to live and work with members of other African tribes whose languages they did not understand. Because of this, the Africans developed a sort of working language that they used to communicate with one another. **Work songs** were one means of communication. These rhythmic group chants helped to provide an outlet for the slaves' vocal expression. They also helped slaves to communicate things such as the master's location, news from neighbors, and other important matters.

The blues developed, in part, from the simple, repetitive strains of these work songs, and it had a great influence on jazz. Jazz used blues' basic structure and **chord progressions** as a starting point, and added improvisation. Jazz also replaced the blues singer with a featured instrumentalist.

Slaves working in the cotton fields of the South.

What does jazz mean? Influential jazz trumpeter Louis Armstrong once said,

" Man, if you have to ask, you'll never know. **"**

The word "jazz" means many things to many people. But the origins of the term itself are still unknown. Some people believe that the word is of African origin and originally meant "to speed up." In musical terms, this described music played with high energy.

During the early 1900s, people couldn't even agree on how to spell the term; "jaz," "jas," and "jass" were all used as alternate spellings before "jazz" became the accepted form.

To further complicate matters, jazz was also a word that described the mood of the music, as well as the state of mind of the jazz musician. In the 1920s, the term came to be used to define an era, the "Jazz Age." It was also used as an adjective to mean something that was cool or fashionable. It's no wonder no two people can agree on exactly what "jazz" means! Its multiple meanings contribute to jazz's longevity as a music genre.

Jazz is Born

Jazz could not have happened anywhere else in the world besides New Orleans, Louisiana. The city's unique mix of cultures had been bubbling since before the United States became a country.

New Orleans was founded as a French port in 1718. In its early years it became the busiest port in North America, with an influx of European, Caribbean, and African cultures intermixing with French settlers. The result was the **Creole** culture. Creole is a rich mix of traditions and art forms including Haitian **voudoun** (**voodoo**), French Catholicism, Cuban musical rhythms and dances, European opera and classical music, and others. The music and frequent celebrations in New Orleans gave it the reputation as a place where the people could *laisser les bon temps rouler*, in French,—"let the good times roll."

The birthplace of jazz: New Orleans in the late 1800s.

The most popular bands at New Orleans celebrations were brass bands. In the late 1800s, the music lovers of New Orleans were more passionate about brass bands than in any other part of of the United States. At New Orleans funerals, brass bands played the somber tunes as the casket was marched toward the cemetery. They then provided the dance music to encourage the friends and family of the departed to celebrate his or her passing by having fun and remembering the good times. The bands' musicians were African Americans and Creoles who were familiar with the African call-and-response form of playing. This became the popular cornerstone of jazz.

The bands specialized in improvisation. Many of the players in these bands could both read music and play by ear, so they could pick up almost any song that was requested of them. If they couldn't, they would "fake it" and improvise. This improvisation essentially created a new song. Improvisation allowed the band members to connect not only with each other, but also with the whims and mood of their audience.

Ragtime

In the late 1800s, a piano style called "ragtime" was developing. Ragtime was a slang term for piano music that featured a syncopated rhythm, and was usually performed by African-American pianists. First among these was Scott Joplin. In 1899, Joplin wrote "The Maple Leaf Rag," one of the first published songs that could be called jazz. Joplin created a composition that increased the tempo (or speed) of dance hall piano pieces of the time. It also demanded more of the player, due to the rhythm of the song. Joplin's ragtime compositions introduced the "groove," or rhythmic feeling, to piano playing of the time.

One of the few surviving photographs of ragtime pioneer Scott Joplin.

Bolden's band

It's difficult to pin down exactly who the first "jazz musician" was. But many people believe it was cornet player and bandleader Charles "Buddy" Bolden.

In the late 1890s, Bolden's band was a top draw in New Orleans. They took their sound from a mix of blues, gospel music, and ragtime, and were known for their habit of upstaging other bands by outplaying them. They were also thought to be the first band to use brass instruments to play the blues. Members of Bolden's band were some of the pioneers of the New Orleans brass bands. Bolden himself was the first of a long line of New Orleans cornet players and bandleaders, such as Freddie Keppard, Joe "King" Oliver, and such well-known artists as Louis Armstrong and Branford Marsalis.

Sadly, in 1907, at the height of the band's success, Bolden had a mental breakdown. Shortly afterwards he was diagnosed with schizophrenia and sent to a mental institution. He remained there until his death in 1931.

The cornet player Buddy Bolder (standing second from left) with fellow musicians. This group was arguably the first-ever jazz band.

New Orleans is Swinging

Even though jazz was being played in the streets and clubs of New Orleans, no recordings were made in the early years. Thomas Edison (1847–1931) invented the phonograph in 1877, but it did not become widely used until 1917, when he created a portable phonograph player for the U.S. Army. The first true jazz recording, by the Original Dixieland Jazz Band, was not made until 1917.

The Original Dixieland Jazz Band made the most of the opportunity, traveling to London and spreading the word about jazz outside the United States. Traveling even farther from New Orleans in 1921 was clarinetist and soprano saxophonist Sidney Bechet. Bechet was a New Orleans teen musical **prodigy** and another of the genre's first generation of ambassadors. Bechet played in Europe as part of Benny Peyton's Jazz Kings and was considered a genius by the European classical musicians who were his hosts and fans.

The Original Dixieland Jazz Band in 1919. The band made the first jazz record.

The legendary Sidney Bechet.

Coleman Hawkins

The tenor saxophonist Coleman Hawkins first became known in the early 1920s as a member of bandleader Fletcher Henderson's orchestra. His playing would eventually change the perception of the saxophone forever, indirectly influencing the course of jazz in the process.

Before Hawkins, the saxophone was mostly used in jazz orchestra settings, and was secondary to the cornet, trumpet, or trombone. But Hawkins' creativity added an energy and "swing" to the instrument that helped it surpass its previous limitations. As a soloist, Hawkins was a peer of cornet player Armstrong and clarinetist Sidney Bechet, both of whom pioneered the jazz "feeling" of their instruments. Hawkins provided an element of usually friendly competition in the New York City jazz scene's cutting contests. In these contests, players would trade solos, often picking up on each other's musical ideas and improving upon them until one or other players gave up.

By 1917, there were a great number of first-generation jazz musicians making a name for themselves in New Orleans. These included Creole pianist Jelly Roll Morton, who claimed to have invented jazz. While this isn't strictly true, Morton's colorful character, as well as his brilliant improvisational piano playing and songwriting, added to his stature as one of the innovators of jazz. His rolling, swinging style influenced generations of jazz piano players for years to come. Morton was one of the first jazz musicians to travel, and take the new sound to places as far as Memphis, Chicago, and California.

Coleman Hawkins, whose revolutionary playing influenced the great saxophone soloists of the future.

One of those players most profoundly affected by Hawkins' transformation of the saxophone was Lester Young. Though Young's style was very different, he too used the sax as a solo instrument. He recorded many important records in the 1930s, and in turn passed Hawkins' mantle to sax innovator Charlie Parker in the 1940s and subsequently to the adventurous John Coltrane in the 1950s and 1960s.

The Jazz Age

The 1920s began with jazz being a minority genre in the South and ended with it providing the soundtrack to the nation's swinging good times. Author F. Scott Fitzgerald (1896–1940), whose famous novel, *The Great Gatsby*, captured the mood of the era, invented the term the "Jazz Age" to describe it.

A key figure in spreading jazz outside New Orleans was Joe "King" Oliver, one of the city's first great cornet players and bandleaders. Oliver's own style was rooted in blues-like sounds and in his own cornet techniques—including his trademark "wah-wah" effect and other expressive innovations. He started his first band in 1907, and by 1921 he had joined in the migration north to industrial cities like Chicago. Indeed it was in Chicago that he launched King Oliver's Creole Jazz Band, whose gigs in Southside Chicago clubs helped bring jazz to an urban environment.

King Oliver's Creole Jazz Band in 1923, featuring (far left) a young Louis Armstrong on slide trombone.

Louis Armstrong

The cornet player Louis Armstrong is a pivotal figure in jazz history. He surpassed Oliver, both in popularity and in the lasting influence he had on jazz music.

Armstrong's playing was quite unlike that of other cornet players of the time. His solos were aggressive, dramatic, and possessed an energy that had not been heard in jazz before. Fans and fellow musicians alike flocked to see him play, and his style set the standard for all jazz soloists, not just cornet players, to this day.

Armstrong left King Oliver's band in 1925 and went on to record the important *Louis Armstrong and His Hot Five* and *Hot Seven*. In these recordings he perfected his solo artistry and pushed both the boundaries of improvisation in jazz, and its popularity, to new limits.

Louis Armstrong brought a new energy into solo playing.

In 1923, King Oliver's Creole Jazz Band, along with well-known artists such as singer Bessie Smith and pianist Jelly Roll Morton, made their first recordings. This was an important moment; until now, no one had kept track of the frequently changing line-ups of jazz bands. Records became historical documents of recording sessions and provided snapshots of the musical chemistry shared by specific players at a specific time. Over the coming years, jazz fans would come to know the work of individual musicians performing on the records. And few would have as big an impact as one young player in King Oliver's Creole Jazz Band: Louis Armstrong.

The Duke

Legendary among the important jazz artists of this period was Duke Ellington. Born in Washington, D.C., he was trained in classical music, but in the early 1920s he began making a name for himself as the leader of five- and six-piece bands in midtown Manhattan clubs. As leader of the Duke Ellington Orchestra, playing the burgeoning Harlem nightclubs, his fame spread.

Between 1926 and 1928, Ellington recorded for virtually every jazz record label, most of which were based in New York City. His impressive live shows mixed sophisticated jazz-pop tunes and show-stopping revue numbers, complete with dancers and singers dressed in flamboyant costumes.

Ellington's instrumentations, arrangements, and style proved hugely influential to the big band and swing music that dominated the 1930s and 1940s.

Duke Ellington (seated at piano) and his orchestra performing "Take the A Train" in the 1943 movie, Reveille With Beverly. The singer is Bette Roche.

As jazz's popularity grew, more and more musicians found their way to New York City. Here they mingled with Broadway theater performers in downtown clubs. But it was uptown, in the neighborhood of Harlem, where jazz really found a home. Harlem was the cultural heart of the city's African-American population. The emergence of jazz here in the 1920s was integral to the **Harlem Renaissance**, an historic outpouring of African-American literature, visual art, theater—and, of course, music. Such notable writers as Zora Neale Hurston and Langston Hughes were among the literary figures who sprang from this explosion of creativity.

The famous Cotton Club in New York's Harlem.

Cab Calloway performing at one of the CBS Radio jazz clubs.

Jazz had two famous homes in Harlem, where the best and brightest musicians performed: the Cotton Club and the Savoy. Both opened in the 1920s to cater to the growing audience for elaborate jazz productions. They were among the first places where big bandleaders such as Duke Ellington, Count Basie, and Cab Calloway, as well as instrumental stars such as Coleman Hawkins, Louis Armstrong, and Sidney Bechet, were introduced to the city's jazz culture. The clubs' stylish décors and fashionable stage shows appealed to the regular audiences, and were also popular with the occasional white Broadway and Hollywood stars that visited the city. The Cotton Club and the Savoy were the places to be seen in the 1920s and 1930s. The Cotton Club has been immortalized in song and film, and the Savoy's place in history was confirmed with Duke Ellington's jazz standard "Stompin' At the Savoy."

Big City Sounds

In the 1930s and 1940s, you could walk down any main street in cities such as New York City, Chicago, and Los Angeles and hear the sounds of big-band jazz. It was a time when the rest of America caught on to jazz and embraced it wholeheartedly. This period was known as the "Swing Era."

Ellington as big-band leader in a stylish poster of the era.

Big-band orchestras were big business in entertainment. They might perform with more than a dozen players, under the direction of bandleaders like Count Basie and Duke Ellington. The Swing Era was also when white bandleaders such as Benny Goodman, Glen Miller, Tommy and Jimmy Dorsey, and Artie Shaw began to attract large audiences. Their wildly popular records were targeted toward white Americans as well as African Americans.

The big-band performing style places less emphasis on improvisation and more on theatrical showmanship and composition. Singers, too, were important. Some of jazz's richest compositions date from this period, including Goodman's "In The Mood," Ellington's "Take the A Train," and Basie's "Basie's Blues."

Benny Goodman's swing band brought jazz to white audiences.

Many of the jazz singers who went on to achieve great fame started with the big bands of the Swing Era. The legendary Frank Sinatra had his first break as a **crooner** with Harry James' big band, and singer Billy Eckstine drew fans to the shows of bandleader Earl Hines.

Female jazz singers featured prominently in big bands, gaining massive popularity in their own right. Ella Fitzgerald started her career as a singer with Chick Webb, while Billie Holiday sang with Benny Goodman. Fitzgerald and Holiday had distinctly different sounds and styles. Fitzgerald's voice could range from high to low notes with ease. She often matched the bouncy mood of the big band with vocal improvisations known as **scat singing**. This style of singing uses made-up words or vocal sounds that directly imitate the sound of saxophones or trumpets and plays off the rhythm of the song. Ella's expressive, warm, and friendly sound even shone through when she was singing a "blues," or sad, song. In later years, she made several famous duet recordings with Louis Armstrong, each joking with the other like a comfortable old couple on songs like "Let's Call the Whole Thing Off."

The peerless jazz duo, Ella Fitzgerald and Louis Armstrong in their later years.

The craze for swing dancing took off in the 1920s, and remained popular through to the 1940s.

From the dawn of the Jazz Age, dancing was an important part of experiencing jazz in the nightclubs. So-called "swing dancing" started in the 1920s in the Cotton Club, the Savoy, and elsewhere, with couples performing energetic dance steps and routines to certain songs. Dances like the "Lindy Hop" became national crazes. The Lindy Hop was named in honor of the famous aviator, Charles Lindberg, and his pioneering flight from New York to Paris in 1927. The craze for dancing to jazz music was helped along by the invention of the jukebox in the 1930s. Jukeboxes gave dancers a chance to practice and boogie even when they weren't out for a big night on the town.

Swing dancing was athletic. Men swung their female partners high into the air or between their legs, and performed gymnastics, like back flips and high kicks. Dancers followed basic steps, but also improvised their own creative moves.

Billie Holiday
singing the
blues in 1943.

The style of the other major female singer of the day, Billie Holiday, was a big contrast to that of Ella Fitzgerald. Although Holiday performed just as many upbeat tunes as Fitzgerald, her voice was full of heartache and world-weariness. She lacked **vocal range**, but her delivery was very expressive, often falling somewhere between speaking and singing.

Neither Holiday nor Fitzgerald led especially happy lives, but while Fitzgerald appeared to sing her blues away, Holiday just sang the blues. Over the course of the 1930s and 1940s her music became increasingly melancholy—witness "Lady Sings the Blues" and "Stormy Monday," with its sad lyrics, *but Tuesday's just as bad..."*

It was this unapologetic honesty that made Holiday's performances all the more gripping, expressing as they did her troubled personal life and descent into drug addiction. She died in 1959 at the age of just 45.

Holiday's style had a marked influence on the great jazz singers Sarah Vaughan and Nina Simone. Elements of the Holiday style can also be heard in the bluesy music of contemporary, Grammy-winning, R&B/jazz artists Alicia Keys and Norah Jones.

One of the most powerful songs of Civil Rights protest came from a nightclub jazz singer known for her songs of heartbreak.

"Strange Fruit" is a haunting depiction of the lynchings of southern African Americans conducted by mobs of white racists. The history of the song begins with a Jewish schoolteacher and union activist from the Bronx, New York, named Abe Meeropol, writing under the pen name Lewis Allan. Meeropol had seen a photograph of lynching victims and was moved to write a poem and basic melody, which became the basis for "Strange Fruit." A mutual friend hand-delivered the song to Billie Holiday.

The opening strains and lyrics convey one of the most vivid images in recording history, made all the more powerful by Holiday's expressive voice.

> *Southern trees bear strange fruit.*
> *Blood on the leaves and*
> *blood at the root.*
> *Black bodies swinging*
> *in the Southern breeze.*
> *Strange fruit hanging*
> *from the poplar trees.*
> (*Strange Fruit* by Lewis Allen)

Holiday's record label refused to record the song, but the singer was so moved by "Strange Fruit" that she recorded and released it herself in 1939 on a tiny independent label. Rarely has a hit record been so haunting, with its shocking depiction of the horrible racism that persisted in the South at that time. Holiday included the song in her set for the next 20 years until her death in 1959.

From Bop to Bebop

In the post–World War II era, jazz underwent a revolution in the way it was both played and perceived. This revolution was called "**bebop**" or simply "bop."

As the 1940s came to a close, the popularity of jazz began to wane. This was because artists had begun to use the genre as a framework for less dance-floor friendly musical experimentation. In the early 1940s, the big bands had been badly affected by a musicians' recording strike and an entertainment tax that had made dance halls less profitable. Paying the dozens of performers was suddenly much more expensive than before. And by the mid-1940s, pop singers such as Frank Sinatra, Bobby Darin, and others were taking big-band jazz into less experimental territory. Throughout its history, jazz had survived because players were willing to change and experiment with the music. So when jazz became almost too safe and predictable during the Swing Era, it clearly needed a fresh approach. This next phase in its evolution was called bop, and it brought improvisation back to jazz.

Bop featured a fast pace and driving rhythms, and emphasized wild solos. It was music designed to be listened to, but not necessarily danced to. Beginning in the early 1940s, such players as John "Dizzy" Gillespie, Charlie "Bird" Parker, and pianist Thelonious Monk were frequenting "after-hours" clubs. These were places they could go after playing their gigs to exchange ideas with other musicians. It was in "**jam sessions**" in such clubs as Minton's Playhouse and Monroe's Uptown House (both in Harlem) that bebop and modern jazz were born. Musicians were free to try out new ideas on an audience of other musicians. It was Gillespie's 1945 recording "Bebop" that gave the movement its name.

Gillespie—who had played in Cab Calloway's showy big band—was bebop's first star. He typically wore thick, black-framed glasses and a beret. The equally expressive, if less personable, Thelonious Monk also helped spread the bebop style. Monk hunched over the piano keyboard looking like he was trying to decide whether or not to play at all before letting loose a series of notes and **riffs** that wowed the crowd. Monk's playing was inventive, and its freedom was attractive to younger musicians who started to adopt the style and spread it among themselves. Jazz was becoming an art form as expressive as any painting.

One of bebop's inventive pioneers, Thelonious Monk, at the piano.

Charlie "Bird" Parker

Like Gillespie, Kansas City-born alto saxophonist Charlie Parker did his time in the world of big bands in the 1940s. But as soon as he started experimenting with smaller groups of three and four players (usually a combination of piano, bass, drums, and trumpet), he found his voice. Parker's playing style was more personal and expressive than that of other saxophonists. He seemed to be playing not out of a need to entertain, but purely to express himself. His style was also rooted in the sound of the blues.

Charlie "Bird" Parker performs at Birdland.

By the late 1940s, Parker's outgoing personality had made him a bebop celebrity. Followers of the new style of jazz flocked to his gigs in New York City and Los Angeles nightclubs. His music was demanding for listeners and also for the musicians who played with him. They had to think on their feet to follow his improvisations and musical ideas. To that end, Parker recruited a band with whom he made some of his most famous recordings, featuring the great drummer Max Roach and a young trumpeter from St. Louis named Miles Davis. Over the next four decades, Davis would become a musical superstar, his fame spreading even outside the jazz world.

By playing gigs at smaller clubs such as Birdland and in coffee houses in Greenwich Village, Parker helped take jazz out of the larger theaters and dance halls to a more intimate audience. Fans of the new jazz became known as "hipsters," derived from the word "hip," a jazz slang term for "good" or "cool."

Cool jazz musician and composer, Dave Brubeck.

Starting in the late 1940s through to the mid-1950s, a new variation on bop emerged in the West Coast cities of San Francisco and Los Angeles. This new style was known as cool jazz. Pianist Dave Brubeck, trumpeter Chet Baker, and saxophonists Stan Getz, Art Pepper, and Lester Young were producing jazz music that smoothed and softened bop's hard edges. This cool jazz style gained a loyal following, especially after the success of Brubeck's bestselling *Take Five*.

Simultaneously, just as Parker's hard bop style was growing in popularity, another form of bop jazz that emphasized funky, soulful grooves began to take shape. "Soul jazz" is a blend of jazz and R&B. Among its pioneers was the Philadelphia organist Jimmy Smith, whose 1956 debut *A New Sound, A New Star* featured an efficient combination of just organ, drums, and guitar. In 1962, pianist and composer Herbie Hancock released the key soul-jazz album *Takin' Off*.

The guitar became a prominent instrument in soul-jazz only as the 1950s came to a close. The funky, **virtuoso** playing of Detroiter Kenny Burrell and Indianapolis-born Wes Montgomery greatly influenced the mainstream jazz that followed, as well as the later playing of **funk** guitarists in the mid- to late-1960s.

The Beat generation

Bebop music was the inspiration for one of the most important literary movements to emerge from the United States— the Beat Generation.

This group of poets and writers, often referred to simply as the Beats, included Jack Kerouac, Allen Ginsberg, William S. Burroughs, and Lawrence Ferlinghetti. They traveled the country, often hitchhiking and hopping trains, seeking out new experiences. In an era when many Americans were settling into comfortable lives in the new suburbs, this was a radically different way of life.

The Beats' writing, especially the **free-form** verse of their poetry, captured the spirit of jazz, and attempted to mimic the improvisation and energy of bebop in particular. It inspired the younger writers, musicians, and artists who would later lead the cultural movements of the 1960s, particularly the hippies. Most famous among beat writers' works were Kerouac's novel *On the Road* and Ginsberg's poem *Howl* (1956).

Beat poet Lawrence Ferlinghetti recites his jazz-inspired verse.

The influence of Latin music like **salsa**, **rumba**, and **cumbia** became increasingly obvious. Toward the end of the bop era, many jazz artists were experimenting with Caribbean and South American rhythms and styles. Dizzy Gillespie once again led the way, while big-band veteran Stan Getz spearheaded the Latin–jazz fusion called Bossa Nova, starting in the early 1960s. In 1963, he teamed up with Brazilian **Tropicalia** stars Antonio Carlos Jobim, João Gilberto, and Gilberto's wife Astrud on the landmark *Getz/Gilberto* album. The sound blended cool jazz and South American styles, with Astrud's enchanting voice delivering such legendary songs as "Girl From Ipanema."

By the end of the 1950s, jazz was everywhere and its styles were incredibly varied. Eventually, experimentation led the music to the brink of what would be called "**avant-garde**" or "free" jazz at the beginning of the 1960s. Bop innovator Thelonious Monk would help create a bridge from the world of bop to the even more experimental world of free jazz.

The Getz/Gilberto team performing in the early 1960s. Stan Getz is left, on saxophone.

Miles Davis and John Coltrane

Two figures tower over the world of jazz from the 1950s on. These are trumpeter and bandleader Miles Davis and tenor saxophonist John Coltrane. The expansion of jazz in the 1950s and beyond would probably have happened without them, but it would not have been nearly as interesting. Both men had a profound influence on jazz's progress. Davis would become the father of jazz fusion and Coltrane of the avant-garde (or free) jazz style.

Miles Davis was born on May 26, 1926. He was the son of a dental surgeon from St. Louis, Missouri, and his parents always supported his musical career. One of the shows they allowed him to see was a local performance by Billy Eckstine's big band, featuring bebop architects Dizzy Gillespie and Charlie Parker. In 1945, Davis moved to New York to study at the famous Juilliard School of Music. However, he also found work as a session musician and ended up quitting school in order to play more. He found work with Eckstine and, soon after, with Charlie Parker. By 1949 Davis was organizing recording sessions for a nine-piece band under his direction. The sessions included horn players Gerry Mulligan, Lee Konitz, and others who would soon help develop the "cool jazz" style. Columbia Records packaged and released the recordings eight years later as the album *Birth of the Cool*.

In 1955, Davis formed his own band. The group made many recordings together, and Davis simultaneously worked with arranger Gil Evans, performing his interpretation of the opera *Porgy and Bess* as well as the gorgeous 1960 release *Sketches of Spain*.

From small group recordings to orchestral performances, Miles Davis attempted it all. His records regularly made it onto the pop charts of the day and his charisma and unpredictable behavior made him the jazz version of an international rock superstar. Many of the important records he made throughout the 1960s were with his Davis Quintet, which included keyboardist Herbie Hancock, saxophonist Wayne Shorter, and bassist Ron Carter. In the late 1960s, Davis began experimenting with rock 'n' roll, and the resulting recordings changed the way jazz interacted with the rock world. *Live-Evil* and *On the Corner* were not only jazz hits—they were pop hits, too.

This photograph of the king of cool, Miles Davis was used on the cover of his 1956 album Round About Midnight.

Doo Bop, recorded in 1991, featured a hip-hop sound, just at a time when hip-hop artists were beginning to incorporate the sounds of jazz into their own music. But time finally caught up with Davis. In September 1991, just before *Doo Bop*'s release, he died of pneumonia at the age of 70. His massive musical talent, along with his adventurous experimentation, have assured that he will always be considered one of the most important figures of jazz music.

Miles Davis had the support of family during his rise to the top, but John Coltrane had a rougher trip to jazz success. The grandson of a preacher, Coltrane grew up in North Carolina with his father and grandparents. When they were killed in a car accident soon after he finished fifth grade, Coltrane moved to Philadelphia to live with his mother and aunts. Coltrane joined his school band and took lessons at a local music school when he was not working to help support the family. By the time he was 19, he had served in the Navy during World War II and returned to Philadelphia to join a local big band. In 1947 he signed with King Kolax's big band and soon made a name for himself.

The first major jazz artist to give John Coltrane a big break was Dizzy Gillespie, who hired him in 1949. Then, in 1955, Miles Davis hired Coltrane (although he would be kicked out in 1957). He played on more than a half-dozen Davis recording sessions for Columbia and Prestige records, before signing with Thelonious Monk's band for a brief stint in 1958. Davis then hired Coltrane back into his band, and Coltrane caught two big breaks. The first was at the 1958 Newport Jazz Festival, where his aggressive, passionate solo style made him a hot topic among jazz critics. Coltrane's other break was in 1959, when he played on Davis' landmark *Kind of Blue* album. The record was hailed as a jazz milestone.

Coltrane finally had the confidence to set out on a solo career in 1960. In the spring of that year, he recorded several albums for the major label Atlantic Records. His version of "My Favorite Things," from the musical *The Sound of Music*, was an unexpected smash hit. Coltrane didn't just cover the song, he reinvented it, making it swing without losing any of its original, innocent charm.

By 1961, two things had changed for Coltrane. Firstly, he was the first artist signed to the new independent label Impulse! Secondly, he had started to play in a style that became known as "free jazz." Free jazz players ignored traditional rules, such as song structure and melody. They were more interested in immediate sound and feeling.

Free jazz supremo,
John Coltrane.

For the next few years, Coltrane alternated between recording traditional-style records for mainstream audiences and playing free-jazz on records like *Africa/Brass* and *Impressions*. During this period he made his best-known record, *A Love Supreme*—a powerful mix of bold, expressive soloing and uplifting arrangements that was born of his renewed interest in religion. The record won him two nominations for Grammy Awards in 1965.

Coltrane recorded furiously for the next year. Then suddenly, in July 1967, he was diagnosed with liver cancer and within two days he had died. Over a period of only seven years as a soloist, Coltrane built up a massive body of work. With his powerful performances, his charismatic personality, his truly innovative techniques, and his devotion to his art, Coltrane's legacy is larger than life.

Avant-Garde Jazz

The avant-garde, or free jazz, of the early 1960s first became well known thanks to the likes of John Coltrane, Ornette Coleman, and bass player Charles Mingus. Mingus' compositions married the roots of jazz, the complexity of classical composition, and the power of orchestral arrangements with free-form playing. His habit of mixing cultures together into something entirely new had a marked influence on such artists and bands as the Art Ensemble of Chicago, Roscoe Mitchell, and Albert Ayler.

Free jazz also had an impact on rock 'n' roll in the mid- to late-1960s. Bands like the MC5 and the Stooges had grown up listening to jazz, rock 'n' roll, and the blues, and their style took something from each. From jazz they took a sense of freedom and lack of stylistic boundaries. When they played live, the MC5 often played extended and improvised jams on their three-minute rock 'n' roll songs. The Stooges also paid close attention to free jazz's experiments with tone and **atonality**. The Grateful Dead, meanwhile, owed much of their group improvisation-based structure to jazz. The Dead were hugely successful, and their loyal cult of fans, nicknamed "Deadheads," followed the band everywhere they went, taping the band's live shows and trading different versions of songs with one another.

Bass player Charles Mingus Blended musical styles to create avant-garde jazz.

Ornette Coleman and free jazz

Many people believe that the free jazz style was the single-handed creation of one man—saxophonist Ornette Coleman. Born in 1930 in Fort Worth, Texas, Coleman bought his first saxophone at age 14, and taught himself how to play. He then played with various R&B and bebop bands before moving to Los Angeles in the early 1950s.

From the beginning Coleman's style was experimental and controversial. He enjoyed mixing up elements of bebop, blues, and funk, but his unorthodox "keening" sounds—or "harmolodics," as Coleman called them—divided the jazz community in the 1950s and 1960s. Some were openly hostile; others hailed him as a genius. Many of his fellow jazz musicians found him difficult to perform with, and some even walked off the stage when Coleman showed up to play.

In 1961, Coleman recorded the album *Free Jazz: A Collective Improvisation*. At 40 minutes, it was the longest jazz recording to date, and also responsible for naming a new jazz genre.

Since then, Coleman has continued to push the boundaries of jazz with his musical experimentations, both solo and with the unusual bands he assembled. One of the most legendary, Prime Time, included two drummers, two guitarists, two bassists, and his own saxophone. The band blended funk rhythms with jazz improvisations. Coleman called this style "free funk." He continued to record well into the mid-1990s.

Ornette Coleman is one of the most notable saxophonists in jazz history.

Jazz Breaks Out

The avant-garde came to its peak with composer and bandleader Sun Ra and his band, the Arkestra. Born Herman Poole Blount, Ra created the myth that his music was delivered from the planet Saturn and was a message to Earth about how to live together in harmony. If that sounded wild, his music was even wilder. The Arkestra wasn't just any large band, it also featured such non-traditional jazz instruments as the oboe, piccolo, the symphonic drum the timpani, and whatever else Ra thought necessary. As the band developed over the course of the early 1960s, Ra began creating improvised pieces on the spot in concert, many of them lasting up to 60 minutes and more. With more than a dozen players, plus vocalists and dancers performing in glittery robes, helmets, and headdresses, it seemed that Ra was indeed from another planet. In the 1970s, Ra's visual presentation and outer space mythology were evident in the stage presentation of fellow space traveler, funk artist George Clinton and his group Parliament/Funkadelic. They began every concert with a landing of the Mothership, a giant spaceship from which the band would enter the stage.

Music from another planet with Sun Ra.

Like blues before it, jazz found its way into rock music. Perhaps the best examples of jazz "fusion" are Miles Davis' early 1970s recordings, which combined the powerful impact of rock 'n' roll and the sophistication of jazz. Bands such as the Indian music-influenced Mahavishnu Orchestra and the sometimes breezy Weather Report followed Davis' lead, and at the end of the 1960s and into the 1970s, many rock acts were bringing jazz into their music.

Also in the late 1960s and early 1970s, Los Angeles guitar player Carlos Santana took influence from his Latino heritage, including **conga** and salsa, and made them work in a rock band with guitar, bass, drums, and keyboards. But Santana's extended group improvisations when he played live made it clear that he also owed a great debt to jazz.

Also in Los Angeles, a guitarist and classically trained composer named Frank Zappa would take jazz's complex song structures and sounds and add them to his own experiments in rock 'n' roll. In 1964, Zappa joined with an R&B band named the Soul Giants, which he renamed the Mothers of Invention. The band went on to attract a devoted cult following that enjoyed both Zappa's unwillingness to compromise his vision in order to make a hit, as well as the zany sense of humor he displayed in his lyrics.

Frank Zappa (second from left) with his Mothers of Invention, whose musical experiments incorporated elements of jazz.

Jazz fusion hit the pop charts in a few different ways. Slick Los Angeles pop band Steely Dan won attention with its smooth blend of laid-back, jazz-influenced rock and biting, dark lyrics. The band Chicago featured a mix of blues, rock, R&B, and jazz, leaning on a horn section that often played arrangements that were heavily influenced by the big-band brass sound of decades earlier. New synthesizer keyboard technology gave both jazz and rock musicians a much broader range of sounds with which to experiment.

By the end of the 1970s, however, jazz fusion and the jazz–rock that sprung from it were so common that they had become somewhat formulaic. Nonetheless the **smooth jazz** style that emerged in the 1980s had some phenomenally successful exponents, such as the multi-platinum selling, North-African singer Sade.

Sade's smooth jazz style propeled her to international superstar.

Rockit

Former Miles Davis sideman and pioneer of the synthesizer in jazz music, Herbie Hancock was also one of the very few jazz musicians to have a hit video on MTV.

Hancock's promotional video for the hip-hop flavored *Rockit* (1983) combined his music's cutting-edge instrumentation, a danceable beat, and visuals of a series of robots engaged in everyday activities from housecleaning to dancing. It was also one of the first pieces of recorded music to feature "scratching." Scratching is when a vinyl record is moved quickly back and forth beneath the stylus in order to produce different sounds. The technique was and still is a staple sound in hip-hop music. At a time when breakdancing was all the rage, scratching helped Hancock become a successful crossover artist when jazz was stuck in a creative slump.

HERBIE HANCOCK
Rockit

Autodrive
Hardrock
Chameleon
Watermelon Man

The cutting-edge album Rockit *pioneered the technique of "scratching" and was promoted with a hit video—a rare thing in jazz.*

Jazz Today

Jazz's expressions have become as varied as its roots. Every style of jazz ever played—from Dixieland to avant-garde and from fusion to big band—is played all over the world. Indeed, jazz is one of this country's most important and enduring cultural exports.

Jazz remains a music that is passed from musician to musician, as in the **oral tradition** of storytelling. While jazz may have long ago peaked in commercial popularity, it still attracts large crowds to festivals around the world. People flock to hear popular artists such as New Orleans'-based trumpeter Wynton Marsalis, who in the 1980s made a conscious effort to return to jazz's roots. By becoming a student of jazz's early Dixieland, big band, and bebop traditions, Marsalis has come to embody the history of the music.

Jazz has found continued life in other ways, too. A modern mix of funk, Latin music, and rhythms, and extended improvisations called funk-jazz (or acid jazz) became popular in the 1980s and 1990s. Furthermore, in the 1990s, jazz was a significant influence on hip-hop via a number bands, including A Tribe Called Quest and Gang Starr. Later, bands such as the Roots and others incorporated jazz's improvisation, complex rhythms, and cool spirit into this other, original American art form.

Wynton Marsalis takes jazz back to its New Orleans roots.

Artists as varied as John Scofield, Norah Jones, Alicia Keys, Brad Meldhau, Josh Redman, and Cassandra Wilson keep the jazz flame alive for a new generation. Other music genres, from rock to R&B, have also benefited from jazz's influence and its ever-changing, adaptable freedom. In this way, jazz will never stay the same, and it will never die.

Norah Jones is among many contemporary artists whose style is indebted to jazz.

In the late 1990s, perhaps as a reaction to the heavy rock 'n' roll and violent hip hop of the time, swing jazz (or, as some had it, "jump blues") made a popular comeback. Bands such as the Squirrel Nut Zippers, Big Bad Voodoo Daddy, the Brian Setzer Orchestra, the Atomic Fireballs were making hits and selling out rock clubs by playing 50-year-old music to fans whose parents may not have even been born the first time swing music was popular.

Along with the swing revival came the swing fashions. Fans wore big-shouldered "zoot suits" and wing-tip shoes. They also used hipster lingo like "daddy-o" and other terms that hadn't been uttered since just after World War II.

But like many popular musical trends based more on style than substance, the swing movement was a distant memory by the year 2000.

Timeline

1619 The first slave ship crosses the Middle Passage
of the Atlantic Ocean.

1861–1865 American Civil War. This war between the
Union and the Confederacy ended in 1865
with the defeat of the Confederates.

1865 Thirteenth Amendment to the U.S. Constitution abolishes slavery.

1877 Invention of the phonograph by Thomas Edison.

1899 Jazz pianist Scott Joplin publishes "Maple Leaf Rag."

1901 Trumpeter and jazz innovator Louis Armstrong is born in New Orleans.

1914–1918 World War I. This war was fought between France,
Britain, and the United States against Germany.
Germany was defeated in 1918. The United States
did not enter the war until 1917.

1917 The Original Dixieland Jazz Band makes the first jazz recording.

1920 Commercial radio broadcasting begins in the United States.

1920-1929 The "Roaring Twenties." This decade is also known
as the "Jazz Age."

1927 The Duke Ellington band begins a four-year residency
at Harlem's The Cotton Club.

1929 The U.S. Stock Market crash begins the period of the 1930s
known as the Great Depression.

1932 Duke Ellington releases the hit song "It Don't mean a Thing
(If It Ain't Got That Swing)."

1939 Singer Billie Holiday releases the anti-lynching song "Strange Fruit."

1941 The United States enters World War II. The war ended in 1945.

1945 Dizzy Gillespie releases his recording "Bebop," giving birth to the jazz genre of the same name.

Late 1940s–1973 Period of U.S. involvement in Vietnam. Involvement in Vietnam in the 1960s through 1973 is commonly called the Vietnam War.

1959 Miles Davis releases *Kind of Blue* featuring saxophonist John Coltrane.
The Dave Brubeck Quartet release their cool jazz album *Time Out*.

1963 Assassination of President John F. Kennedy on November 22nd.

1964 Civil Rights Act is signed by President Lyndon B. Johnson.

1967 John Coltrane dies.

1968 Assassination of African-American Civil Rights leader, Martin Luther King Jr. in April.
Assassination of presidential candidate Robert F. Kennedy, brother of late President John F. Kennedy in June.

1983 Herbie Hancock releases *Rockit*.

Glossary

atonality describes a piece of music that varies from traditional

avant-garde group of people, in this case musicians, who develop and promote new ideas in an art form

bebop jazz style started in the early 1940s that stresses fast tempos and improvisation

call-and-response when the leader of a group and the chorus or other members of the group alternate performing parts of a song

chord progression sequence of chords performed in a piece of music

conga Latin American dance music where the dancers form a line that moves to the rhythm of the conga drum

Creole someone of mixed descent — in this case, usually a mixture of Latino, French, and African; also the culture that emerges from these mixed races

crooner smooth, gentle style of romantic singing from the big band era

cumbia a dance rhythm similar to salsa, originating in Colombia

free-form music or poetry that is free from typical structures

funk American style of music derived from R&B which emphasizes a prominent, persistent beat

Harlem Renaissance period from around 1920 to 1940 in which African-American artistic culture blossomed in the New York City neighborhood of Harlem

improvise performing a piece or portion of music without prior preparation

jam session when musicians play together in impromptu ensenbles

oral tradition folk method by which songs and stories are passed orally from generation to generation without being written down

polyrhythm literally more than one rhythm. The combination of two or more often contrasting rhythms

prodigy very young, talented musician

rumba music, developed in the early 1900s, that accompanies the Cuban dance of the same name

riff repeated chord progression, often played by the rhythm section.

salsa Caribbean folk dance music started in Cuba that spread to Puerto Rico and New York City in the mid 1900s

scat singing style of singing in which percussive and nonsense sounds and words are used to imitate the sound of musical instruments

smooth jazz blending of jazz and pop music originating in the 1980s

syncopation momentary pause or displacement of the beat for dynamic effect

Tropicalia Brazilian pop music from the 1960s influenced by American jazz and folk

virtuoso exceptionally skilled musician or performer

vocal range range of notes, from low to high, that a singer can sing

voudon (or voodoo) religion based on pagan gods and the worship of dead ancestors

work songs songs sung in unison by groups of slaves and prisoners to pass the time while working, during the slavery and Reconstruction period in the American South

Further Information

WEBSITES

Smithsonian Music resources:

www.si.edu/resource/faq/nmah/music.htm

PLACES TO VISIT

American Jazz Museum

1616 E. 18th St.

Kansas City, MO 64108

816-474-8463

Email: ajm@kcjazz.org

www.americanjazzmuseum.com

Preservation Hall

726 Saint Peter St.

New Orleans, LA 70116

504-523-8939

A sort of "living museum" with nightly
performances of old-time New Orleans jazz.

Experience Music Project

325 5th Ave. N.

Seattle, WA 98109

877-367-5483

www.emplive.org

Huge interactive music museum and archive.
Covers all types of popular music—jazz,
soul/R& B, rock, country, folk, and blues.

Rock and Roll Hall of Fame Museum

One Key Plaza

751 Erieside Ave

Cleveland, OH 44114

216-781-ROCK

www.rockhall.com

Huge museum that covers not only rock, but
folk, country, R&B, blues, and jazz.

RECORDINGS

Duke Ellington:

Ellington at Newport 1956 (live)

(Sony)

Louis Armstrong:

The Essential Louis Armstrong

(Sony)

Billie Holiday:

Lady Day: The Best of Billie Holiday

(Sony)

Miles Davis:

Sketches of Spain

(Sony)

Charlie Parker:

The Essential Charlie Parker

(Polygram Records)

John Coltrane:

A Love Supreme

(Impulse Records)

Thelonious Monk:

Monk's Dream

(Sony)

Stan Getz:

Getz/Gilberto

(Polygram Records)

Dave Brubeck:

Time Out

(Sony)

Index